'The Little Him Book is an introduction to the roles of Jesus and gives a glimpse into who He is and what He has done for us. It serves as a wonderful catalyst for a quiet time that will renew your appreciation for all God has done for His own.'

Darrell L. Bock, Senior Research Professor of New Testament Studies, Dallas Theological Seminary

'This is a remarkable little book. It brings together the major identities of Jesus of Nazareth in a creative and unique way. Peter Mead has done a service for all of us who long to understand Jesus more deeply.'

Michael Card, Bible teacher and musician

'Peter Mead does a wonderful job of distilling vast and powerful truths into a format which quickly draws you in and stirs your heart. The only fitting response to the reality of Jesus is to worship, and it is just that which this book resources the reader to do through Scripture, exposition and carefully chosen hymns.'

Nathan Fellingham, musician and song-writer

'Has your heart grown cold towards Christ? Do you find it hard to sing to Him? This little firecracker of a book combines rich theology, heartwarming truths and a hymn at the end of every chapter that gives you space to worship and praise Him!'

Olly Knight, Worship Team Leader,
The City Church, Canterbury

'The Little Him Book is a thoroughly enjoyable, Christ-centered book that inspires love and worship for our wonderful Saviour. It only takes a little book to extol Jesus in such a way that your heart and mind will desire Him.'

Zefjan Nikolla, BSKSH / IFES Albania

'This delightful book will bring cool water to your soul as you learn to see Jesus through new eyes. Peter Mead captures the insights of a scholar and weaves them into your heart with the winsome words of a shepherd. The combination of depth and delight will give you a deeper love for your master and transformation for your soul. It is a must-read for every follower of Jesus!'

Dave Patty, Josiah Venture

'Instead of giving us ten steps for self-improvement, Peter Mead gives us ten fresh views of Christ to lift our hearts and our perspective. It's like a holiday in the Caribbean for the soul: warm, refreshing, wonderful!'

Michael Reeves, President, Union School of Theology

'This short book has a sweet message: Jesus is everything you need in every way. The Little Him Book takes you on a journey through the Bible to meet Jesus afresh, and the view is stunning.'

Jonathan Thomas, Pastor, Cornerstone Church, Abergavenny

'As our understanding of Christ deepens, so does our praise and adoration of him. This short book assists us to do both. Peter Mead unpacks some of the main attributes and titles of Christ in an engaging and accessible way. He enables the reader to grasp deep spiritual truths with such clarity that you won't feel overwhelmed by words but overwhelmed with wonder! That same wonder draws us to worship. It is appropriate therefore, that words from some of the greatest hymns ever penned furnish each chapter with a helpful response to all that we have read. The illustrative material, the Scripture passages, *reflections, questions and Hymns make this a superb devotional book, and one which I trust will achieve everything the author intended.'*

Colin Webster, Minister, Cornerstone Church, Nottingham

THE LITTLE
HIM BOOK

LOOKING AT THE JESUS WHO
MAKES OUR HEARTS SING

PETER MEAD

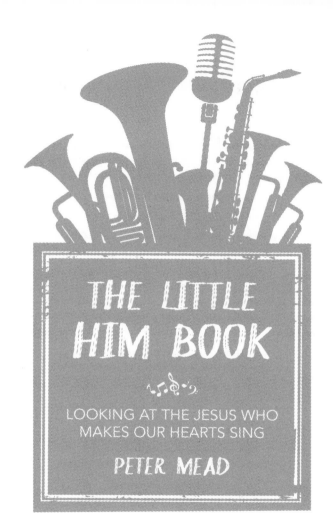

THE LITTLE HIM BOOK

LOOKING AT THE JESUS WHO
MAKES OUR HEARTS SING

PETER MEAD

Copyright © 2020 by Peter Mead

First published in Great Britain in 2020

The right of Peter Mead to be identified as the Author of this Work has been asserted by him in accordance with the Copyright, Designs and Patents Act 1988.

British Library Cataloguing in Publication Data
A record for this book is available from the British Library

ISBN: 978-1-913278-38-0

Designed and typeset by Pete Barnsley (CreativeHoot.com)

Printed in Denmark by Nørhaven

10Publishing, a division of 10ofthose.com
Unit C, Tomlinson Road, Leyland, PR25 2DY, England

Email: info@10ofthose.com
Website: www.10ofthose.com

1 3 5 7 10 8 6 4 2

CONTENTS

The Little Him Book..1

1. The Son...7

2. The Deliverer 17

3. The Baby 25

4. The Storyteller 33

5. The Miracle-Worker 43

6. The Missionary 51

7. The King...61

8. The Brother..69

9. The Bridegroom 79

10. The Rest of the Story..............................89

Be Thou My Vision......................................95

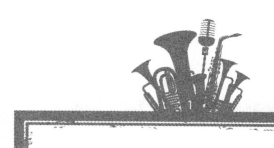

THE LITTLE HIM BOOK

*'Remove Christ from the Scriptures
and there is nothing left.'*
Martin Luther

This is not a book about *hymns* – it is a book about *him*. Christianity is about Christ. One of the most famous verses in the Bible declares that God loved, and God gave so that if we believe in the one God gave, we will have eternal life. And yet, while we may be familiar with the words of John 3:16, often its truth fails to grip our hearts. After all, many people don't think that God is loving and giving; isn't he demanding and impossible to please? And what does it mean to 'believe in' Jesus anyway?

Earlier in John 3, Jesus is talking with Nicodemus, a man at the top of the social totem pole. He is educated, he is influential, he is impressive. But Jesus tells him that unless he begins life from scratch – until he is born again by the Spirit of God – he can't even begin to understand what life is all about. So how can Nicodemus, who Jesus is speaking with (or any of the rest of us) gain access to this new life from the Spirit of God?

Jesus points him back to a story from the days of Moses. The people of Israel were camped in a place where many of them were being killed by deadly snakes. They cried out to God for help, and he instructed Moses to make a bronze snake skewered by a spear and lift it up. (This may sound strange to our twenty-first-century ears – but those listening to Jesus would have been reminded of God's great promise that he would crush the head of the serpent that had originally led humanity into rebellion against him.) When the people were bitten by the snakes, the instruction was simple: don't try to suck out the poison, don't try to find a nurse or look for an ancient ambulance, just look at the snake on the spear. Look and live. It was an act of absolute trust. In fact, it was a non-act. Do nothing. If you try, you die.

So, Jesus told Nicodemus, 'Just as Moses lifted up the snake in the wilderness, so the Son of Man must be lifted up, that everyone who believes may have eternal life in him' (Jn. 3:14–15). To believe in Jesus is not about *doing* something: we are not supposed to make resolutions, turn over new leaves or fix our ways. To believe in Jesus is to simply look and live – that is, to fix the gaze of our hearts on the one who was lifted up for us. It is an act of absolute trust. But really, like the Israelites in the desert, it is a non-act. Do nothing. Just look and live.

The only way to become a Christian is to place all your trust in Jesus – in who he is and what he has done. And the only way to grow consistently as a Christian is to keep the gaze of your heart fixed on Jesus.

The best forms of Christianity have always made much of Christ. Christianity without Christ at the centre is an anomaly. It doesn't make sense. And yet, throughout history many have drifted away from a central focus on Christ. Perhaps lazy theology creeps in, and God is treated as a generic deity instead of the Trinity of true Christianity. Or perhaps emphasis is placed on Jesus' mother, Mary, and suddenly biblical references to Christ's saving work are wrongly attributed to her. Or perhaps the Holy Spirit's role of pointing us to Christ is replaced by something more self-centred, such as making his main role to empower me for my ministry. Maybe we simply get caught up with ourselves again, just like we were before we were saved. How easily Christianity can lose Christ; how easily he can become a mere resource to get our prayers answered, or a sculpted figure to venerate.

This little book has one simple aim: to nudge you to think about Jesus – more than that, to find him at the centre of your identity, your worship, your affections and your life. Whether this is your first exposure to Jesus, or you have known him for years, this little book is all about getting to know Jesus better and delighting in him more.

While each chapter is short, it will hopefully stir thoughts that can be pondered at length. Each chapter will conclude with a Bible passage, a couple of questions, and a song you might like to sing or meditate on. For centuries, Jesus has stirred his followers to burst into songs of worship, adoration and devotion.

May we truly live with Jesus as the centre of everything. May it be your growing experience to live with the very gaze of your soul fixed on him and your heart singing in delight because of all that you see!

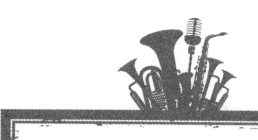

THE SON

Jesus has many titles scattered throughout the Bible, all of which point to some aspect of his person or mission. He is the great prophet, priest and king. He is Immanuel, the Saviour of the world, the Lion of Judah, the Servant of Yahweh, the Lord of Glory, the Alpha and the Omega, the Word, the Light of the World, the Nazarene, the Bridegroom, the Great and Good Shepherd, the King of kings, and Lord of lords, the Christ, and dozens more. We could ponder all of these at length, and we will spend time with some of them later in this book. But let's start here. Of all his titles, none offers more for us to unpack than this: the Son.

To say that Jesus is the Son is to begin before the beginning. Before anything had been created, before there was anything that needed to be ruled, what existed? The Bible tells us that, in the beginning, there was God. Here we have to be careful. It is easy for us to think of a solitary being thinking about himself. That is because we are fallen sinners who are used to thinking about ourselves as more important than everyone else. Actually, the Bible reveals a far more thrilling glimpse into eternity past.

In John 17, Jesus is praying to his Father just before he is arrested, tried and killed. Look at these words and see what they reveal about the eternity that is beyond our time:

> 'Father, the hour has come. Glorify your Son, that your Son may glorify you. For you granted him authority over all people that he might give eternal life to all those you have given him. Now this is eternal life: that they know you, the only true God, and Jesus Christ, whom you have sent. I have brought you glory on earth by finishing the work you gave me to do. And now, Father, glorify me in your presence with the glory I had with you before the world

began. I have revealed you to those whom you gave me out of the world' (Jn. 17:1b–6).

'I have given them the glory that you gave me, that they may be one as we are one – I in them and you in me – so that they may be brought to complete unity. Then the world will know that you sent me and have loved them even as you have loved me. Father, I want those you have given me to be with me where I am, and to see my glory, the glory you have given me because you loved me before the creation of the world' (Jn. 17:22–24).

The whole prayer is incredibly revealing, but even in just these few verses, notice what we are told about the eternal realm of God's glory. We see that glory is given by the Father to the Son, and then by the Son to the Father. The Son is the 'revealer' of the Father, and what he reveals is a beautiful, love-driven glory giving that was forever there, even before the world was created. To say that Jesus is the Son is a glimpse into something truly wonderful. He is the Son because there is a Father, and their relationship is vibrant and loving. And, amazingly, their relationship is now being shared with us!

Before there was anything else, there was a Father loving his Son, and the Son responding in love to his Father. This Father and Son were forever glorifying each other by the Spirit who united them perfectly as one. This is the God of Christianity – the Father and Son united in perfect harmony by the Spirit. Three persons, one God. This is a tri-unity or, if you push the words together, the Trinity.

Do not get discouraged by your mathematical inability to do the sums, the Trinity is not a mathematical conundrum. The Trinity is the most delightful and thrilling reality. For thousands of years, humans have generated all sorts of alternative gods, but none of them are anywhere near as thrilling as the one true God, the Trinity.

We do not have space to plumb the depths of the richness of the Trinity, but let's scratch the surface and briefly introduce each person in the Trinity. In Paul's letter to the Ephesians, he begins with a description of the Trinity at work in our salvation.

Praise be to the God and Father of our Lord Jesus Christ, who has blessed us in the heavenly realms with every spiritual blessing in Christ. For he chose us in him before the creation of the world to be holy and blameless in his sight. In love he predestined us for adoption to sonship through Jesus Christ, in accordance with his pleasure and will – to the praise of his glorious grace, which he has freely given us in the One he loves. In him we have redemption through his blood, the forgiveness of sins, in accordance with the riches of God's grace that he lavished on us. With all wisdom and understanding, he made known to us the mystery of his will according to his good pleasure, which he purposed in Christ, to be put into effect when the times reach their fulfilment – to bring unity to all things in heaven and on earth under Christ.

In him we were also chosen, having been predestined according to the plan of him who works out everything in conformity with the purpose of his will, in order that we, who were the first to put our hope in Christ, might be

> *for the praise of his glory. And you also were*
> *included in Christ when you heard the message*
> *of truth, the gospel of your salvation. When*
> *you believed, you were marked in him with*
> *a seal, the promised Holy Spirit, who is a*
> *deposit guaranteeing our inheritance until the*
> *redemption of those who are God's possession –*
> *to the praise of his glory (Eph. 1:3–14).*

First, the Father is the one who blesses us, who chooses us, who initiates, who has plans 'in accordance with his pleasure and will' (v. 5). When we speak about the will of God, it is the Father's plans that we are describing. God has eternal purposes to work out, and verse 6 tells us that these plans are going to lead 'to the praise of his glorious grace'.

The Father's purposes are worked out by sending his Son into his creation. In verses 7–12, Paul explains that the Son has bought us back with his blood and will one day unite all things under his rule. After the Son, then the Father sends forth his Spirit – see verses 13–14, where Paul describes how the Spirit is the guarantee of all that we are to receive in Christ.

So, the Son is the forever 'revealer' of the Father. If we want to know what God is like, we need only look to the Son, who perfectly represents the Father (Jn. 14:7). The Son is also the Saviour sent into our world to work out God the Father's gracious plan to rescue and redeem us by the shedding of his blood (Eph. 1:7). The Son's obedience to the Father's plan is perfect, and the Father's desire is to bring everything together in the Son, because it is the Son who is to be at the centre of everything (Eph. 1:10).

The Holy Spirit is sent forth to communicate the heart of the Father by pointing sinners to the Son, so that they can see the Father in Jesus (Jn. 15:26; 16:14). The Spirit is the great communicator. He seems to be the very love of the Father and Son communicated back and forth, then spilling out toward us in God's good plans. The Spirit never competes with the Son, but instead always points us towards Jesus. He confirms and reassures us that we belong to Christ until the day when we are forever with him.

The good news of Christianity is *great* news because of who God is. We are invited into the loving fellowship of the Trinity. Actually, there is no Christianity without the Trinity – you simply cannot give an adequate explanation of the good news, the gospel, without all three persons of the Trinity working together perfectly.

So the Son reveals the Father's heart-desire to save sinful humanity. When we start to grasp the Son's role in the Trinity, we find great comfort. Why? Because we have a God who is not hiding; he can be known. We are not dealing with a distant and dark deity that hides away from mere mortals like us. We have a God who can be known in and through his Son. Not only does Jesus reveal the Father's loving heart to us, but Jesus also makes it possible for sinners like us to be brought into the loving community of the Trinity.

Jesus, the Son, reveals God's heart to us. Think about Jesus making God known, and know the comfort that can only come from the great assurance that God truly loves you.

A PASSAGE TO PONDER: EPHESIANS 1

The first part of this chapter, from verses 3–14, states that everything God has done is 'to the praise of his glorious grace'. What have the Father, the Son and the Spirit done for you, according to these verses?

The second part of the chapter, from verses 15–23, is a prayer that Paul prayed for the Ephesian believers to grow closer to God. Why not pray that the truths in that prayer would grip your heart more and more as you read your Bible (and as you read this book).

A SONG TO SING

Blessed assurance, Jesus is mine!
O what a foretaste of glory divine!
Heir of salvation, purchase of God,
Born of His Spirit, washed in His blood.

This is my story, this is my song,
Praising my Saviour, all the day long;
This is my story, this is my song,
Praising my Saviour, all the day long.

Perfect submission, perfect delight,
Visions of rapture now burst on my
sight;
Angels descending bring from above
Echoes of mercy, whispers of love.

This is my story, this is my song…

Perfect submission, all is at rest
I in my Saviour am happy and blest,
Watching and waiting, looking above,
Filled with His goodness, lost in His love.

This is my story, this is my song…

Fanny Crosby, 1820—1902

THE DELIVERER

Out of the spreading goodness of God's giving nature flowed creation (see Genesis 1 – 2) ... and then, redemption (see the rest of the Bible)! His creation was gloriously diverse and united in perfection, with God's image-bearers (humans) representing his loving rule to all the creatures. However, the first couple did not represent God well. Already in the third chapter of Genesis, we find Eve in a slippery conversation with the crafty serpent:

> 'You will not certainly die,' the serpent said
> to the woman. 'For God knows that when you
> eat from it your eyes will be opened, and you
> will be like God, knowing good and evil.'

When the woman saw that the fruit of the tree was good for food and pleasing to the eye, and also desirable for gaining wisdom, she took some and ate it. She also gave some to her husband, who was with her, and he ate it. Then the eyes of both of them were opened, and they realized they were naked; so they sewed fig leaves together and made coverings for themselves (Gen. 3:4–7).

The cunning serpent easily led them astray into disbelieving God's Word and turning their love away from God and onto themselves. They turned from the good God to a different kind of goodness – a self-defined goodness wrapped up in being self-loving mini gods.

Adam and Eve took the fruit of the tree of the knowledge of good and evil. But, until that point, all they had known was good, good, good. So effectively, the only thing that they added to their first-hand knowledge of good was this: evil. They were sold the lie that they would be like God, but instead of becoming deities, they discovered only the disappointing inadequacy of their own nakedness.

Here is the tricky thing about being fallen: we are utterly inadequate, and yet we cling to the nonsense that we can do something about it by covering up that inadequacy and shame with fig leaves! You probably don't have fig leaf garments in your wardrobe, but we all default to presenting ourselves with our inadequacies carefully concealed!

Adam and Eve instinctively covered themselves as soon as they became sinfully self-aware. God then walked into the garden to speak with them. They had swallowed the great lie about becoming like God, but now God wanted to offer some clarity to them. He told them of the consequences of their sin. He demonstrated the price of sin by providing garments of death to cover their woefully inadequate and naked bodies (Gen. 3:21). And he promised them a deliverer:

> So the Lord God said to the serpent, 'Because you have done this,
>> Cursed are you above all livestock
>> and all wild animals!
> You will crawl on your belly

> *and you will eat dust*
> *all the days of your life.*
> *And I will put enmity*
> *between you and the woman,*
> *and between your offspring and hers;*
> *he will crush your head,*
> *and you will strike his heel'*
> *(Gen. 3:14–15).*

The great consequence of sin is death. But God promised that death itself would one day be reversed by a male child of a woman. God was so in charge that he could promise the resolution to the human problem – the resolution was a promise that a human would deliver humanity from sin. Which man would crush the serpent's head? Surely humans had proved to be inadequate against the serpent? Indeed they had, but God was promising a solution that would come from beyond ourselves and yet would be one of us.

As we read on through the Old Testament, we discover more and more detail about this coming deliverer: he would be descended from Shem, from Abram, from Isaac, from Jacob, from Judah, then later from Jesse, and from

David (Gen. 12:1–7; 26:3–4; 28:13–14; 49:10; 2 Sam. 7:12–16). God revealed his plans ahead of time, and yet the great serpent, Satan, could never thwart that plan. The scarlet thread of divine promise winds through the messy pages of human failure that is the Old Testament. A male child was coming who would be one of us, and yet the promise was from beyond us, from this God who continued to reveal himself to key characters in the story.

God didn't just ask them to trust a promise, he asked them to trust him, the Promiser. It was this Promiser – the Son who reveals the Father – who walked into the garden to bring hope to Adam and Eve (Jn. 1:18; Gen. 3:8). It was this Promiser who met with Abraham, with Isaac, with Moses, with Gideon and with Solomon, and who Isaiah saw on the heavenly throne (eg. Gen. 12:7; Ex. 33:11; Is. 6:1). Ultimately, it was this Promiser who became one of us forever and is the great promised answer to our greatest problem.

It is the promise of the Deliverer, as well as the presence of the Promiser, which give us infinite hope in the mess of our lives. Thank God that he was strong enough to defeat sin with a human, and he was gracious enough to become that human for us. We can never solve our greatest problem. But we have a solution which comes from outside of ourselves. Our great hope is the man, Christ Jesus!

As we spend time thinking about the thousands of years of preparation for the coming of the Deliverer, let it stir great hope within you. God knows you cannot fix the mess that is inside you, but do *you* know it? The solution you need has to come from beyond yourself. Praise God that he provided that solution by sending the Son to become like you and rescue you. Our human hearts keep defaulting back to the nonsense that we can sort ourselves out. Listen for the hiss of the serpent and spot the lie – you are not a god, you need God! We cannot fix ourselves, and God knows it. It is only in Jesus that we have the answer to our own deepest needs.

A PASSAGE TO PONDER: PSALM 32

Compare what the psalm says about the person living under the weight of unconfessed sin with the person whose sin is forgiven. Take some time to talk to God about your sin and his unfailing love.

This psalm was written a thousand years before Jesus came to do the work of deliverance on the cross. Think about the way that every truth in this psalm makes so much more sense for us in light of all that Jesus did that first Easter.

A SONG TO SING

Amazing grace! How sweet the sound
That saved a wretch like me!
I once was lost, but now am found;
Was blind, but now I see.

'Twas grace that taught my heart to fear,
And grace my fears relieved;
How precious did that grace appear
The hour I first believed.

Through many dangers, toils and snares,
I have already come;
'Tis grace hath brought me safe thus far,
And grace will lead me home.

The Lord has promised good to me,
His word my hope secures;
He will my shield and portion be,
As long as life endures.

Yea, when this flesh and heart shall fail,
And mortal life shall cease,
I shall possess, within the veil,
A life of joy and peace.

The world shall soon dissolve like snow,
The sun forbear to shine;
But God, who called me here below,
Shall be forever mine.

When we've been there ten thousand years,
Bright shining as the sun,
We've no less days to sing God's praise
Than when we'd first begun.

John Newton, 1725—1807

THE BABY

After the centuries of anticipation that we see in the Old Testament, we cross the blank page into the New Testament and find ourselves confronted with a Christmas card story. Surely this is some sort of fairy tale? A stable, a young unmarried couple, a baby laid in a manger, shepherds, wise men …

This is no fairy tale. This is God the Son stepping into our world. At this pivotal moment in history, we would expect fanfares and military might, but instead God arrived quietly in the humblest of circumstances. Matthew's account of the Christmas story begins and ends with two key names for Jesus: Immanuel and the Nazarene. Both speak of the same thing: Jesus is one of us. Although he is God himself, he came and lived among us; although he is God, he lived in an insignificant and very normal place (Matt. 1:23; 2:23).

Matthew begins his gospel with the genealogy of Jesus that wends its way through the highs and lows of the Old Testament family tree; from Abraham, to David, and all the way to the time when the New Covenant was promised and the exile began. At the same time, this list of names includes surprising participants who nobody would expect to see listed in the family line of the Messiah: Tamar, Rahab, Ruth, Bathsheba – four women with question marks over their sexual integrity. These four set up the final woman in the list, Joseph's wife-to-be, Mary, whose baby bump was starting to show (Matt. 1:1–17).

But then comes the story of God announcing his plans to Joseph. Mary, his wife-to-be, was not to be cast aside. Actually, the baby was there by the Holy Spirit. This was all very well, but Joseph and Mary would still have to face the disbelieving faces of their neighbours as they sought to live their lives in the years to come. Who would ever trust Joseph in business if he insisted that the baby was conceived miraculously and that neither of them were 'sinners' like so many others in Nazareth? But Joseph trusted God. And ultimately, both Mary and Joseph were to trust in the baby himself, for he was Immanuel, which means, 'God with us' (Matt. 1:18–25).

Jesus became 'God with us' in our sinful world. He was 'God with us' in the mess of broken lives, broken promises and shattered dreams. He did this not only to empathise but, more importantly, to save us from our sins. So, although he was definitely Immanuel, God with us, Mary and Joseph actually named him Jesus – which means, 'the Lord saves!' – as the angel had instructed them.

As Matthew continues to tell the story of Jesus' birth, we discover that he came to save not only Jews, but people from other nations too. We also discover how much Satan hated Jesus' birth and worked through Herod the Great to seek his immediate destruction. Yet God delivered his Son via an escape to Egypt. And finally, the story ends with us being introduced to a bizarre label – this Jesus would be called a Nazarene:

After Herod died, an angel of the Lord appeared in a dream to Joseph in Egypt and said, 'Get up, take the child and his mother and go to the land of Israel, for those who were trying to take the child's life are dead.'

So he got up, took the child and his mother and went to the land of Israel. But when he heard that Archelaus was reigning in Judea in place of his father Herod, he was afraid to go there. Having been warned in a dream, he withdrew to the district of Galilee, and he went and lived in a town called Nazareth. So was fulfilled what was said through the prophets, that he would be called a Nazarene (Matt. 2:19–23).

It is not difficult to understand why Joseph was inclined to return to Bethlehem in Judea instead of Nazareth – there would be far fewer wagging tongues and knowing looks. It is also not hard to understand why the presence of Archelaus reigning in Judea in place of his father Herod compelled Joseph to choose Nazareth in Galilee after all. The history books tell us that Archelaus was both corrupt and violent, a real chip off the old block. What is difficult to understand is what Matthew means when he says that Jesus growing up in Nazareth and being called a Nazarene was a fulfilment of prophecy.

There is no clear Old Testament prophetic reference to make sense of this, although there are a couple of possible options. For the sake of space, let's simply note that, throughout chapter 2, Matthew seems to be pointing to fulfilments of prophecy related to places (Matt. 2:5–6, 15, 18, 23).

What, then, is the significance of Nazareth? Nazareth was a nowhere town in Galilee. Surely Jesus should be known as the Bethlehemite, for that was the prophesied town of his birth? No. Jesus would be nicknamed 'the Nazarene'. Jesus came to live in and be from Nazareth, in other words, 'Nowhere, Galilee'. That is, he truly came to be Immanuel – God with us. He didn't come just to be God near us safely living in a nice sterile palace. No, Jesus was truly God with us, in Nowhere, Wiltshire, or Nowhere, Hungary, or Nowhere, Nebraska. He came to live among us and to identify with us:

an ordinary person, living an ordinary life in an ordinary town – with us.

Incidentally, it is so encouraging that Jesus continues to be called 'the Nazarene' throughout his ministry career, and even after he has ascended and is back at his true home address – heaven itself. Our Saviour is the Nazarene because God was serious about being Immanuel; he was serious about being with us. Not only do we have access to God the Father's heart as it is revealed perfectly in the Son, but the Father has perfect access to our hearts. Why? Because in Jesus, Immanuel, the Nazarene, we have the assurance of being understood. He knows exactly what it is like to be a human, to deal with human experiences, temptations and emotions. Jesus became one of us, and he knows us – and that can bring a great assurance to our relationship with a God we do not see. He sees us, he knows us, and there is someone just like us, from Nowhere, Galilee, sitting at the Father's right hand and speaking for us.

A PASSAGE TO PONDER: JOHN 1:1-18

John did not choose to begin his gospel with the birth of Jesus, but with a soaring introduction to Jesus as the Word who was always at the Father's side and yet became one of us. Carefully read through this passage and notice everything it says about Jesus.

In light of this passage, think again about the Christmas story that we have been reading about in this chapter. What stirs your heart to worship Jesus more: the heavenly realities of John 1 or the humble realities of that first Christmas?

A SONG TO SING

Hark! the herald angels sing,
'Glory to the new-born King!
Peace on earth, and mercy mild,
God and sinners reconciled.'
Joyful, all ye nations, rise,
Join the triumph of the skies;
With th'angelic host proclaim,
'Christ is born in Bethlehem.'

Hark! the herald angels sing,
'Glory to the new-born King!'

Christ, by highest heaven adored:
Christ, the everlasting Lord;
Late in time behold him come,
Offspring of a virgin's womb.
Veiled in flesh, the Godhead see;
Hail, th'incarnate Deity:
Pleased, as man, with man to dwell,
Jesus, our Emmanuel!
Hark! the herald angels sing,
'Glory to the new-born King!'

Hail! the heaven-born Prince of peace!
Hail! the Son of Righteousness!
Light and life to all he brings,
Risen with healing in his wings
Mild he lays his glory by,
Born that man no more may die:
Born to raise the sons of earth,
Born to give them second birth.
Hark! the herald angels sing,
'Glory to the new-born King!'

Charles Wesley, 1707—1788

THE STORYTELLER

Jesus told stories, and he told them really well. He could captivate an audience. He could both infuriate religious opponents and encourage common uneducated folks, all with the same story. Jesus spoke with an authority that the educated elite could neither emulate nor explain. He had created the cosmos, and yet he spoke in simple little stories that were vivid and gripping.

To fully appreciate Jesus as a storyteller, we have to recognise his divided audience. There were the religious leader types – the Pharisees and the Scribes, and so on. They were the educated folks, but more importantly, they were supposedly the 'good' people. Then there were the common folks. Included in this group were an uncomfortably high number of prostitutes, tax collectors, and other categories of sinners – the 'bad' people.

Jesus told parables. Perhaps you've heard the old pithy explanation that a parable is an earthly story with a heavenly meaning? Do not take this to mean simple stories with profound and yet understandable meanings. The religious elite, for instance, seemed oblivious to the heavenly meanings! And Jesus overtly said that he told his stories so the hard-hearted would *not* understand.

One time, Jesus was confronted by a Sadducee who wanted to trap Jesus with a complex comedic tragedy about a woman who married seven brothers, one after the other (Lk. 20:27–40). Perhaps something in her falafel killed them all off one by one! So, in the resurrection, the Sadducee wanted to know, who would she be married to? Jesus undid this story trap with the expertise of a master bomb-disposal expert – he pointed the Sadducee (who didn't believe in angels or eternity) to angels and their marriage-less state in eternity. While the Sadducee must have been infuriated with this answer, the onlookers would have probably enjoyed the spectacle!

However, most of Jesus' work with stories was not about undoing the stories, but much more to do with telling them. And when he did, he often undid his listeners in the process.

Let's take a famous one for instance. In Luke 15, Jesus was being criticised for partying with sinners, so he told a triple-layered parable. He started with two little stories to set the scene: A man followed by a woman. He lost a sheep; she lost a coin. They found their lost items and they partied. Then came the main story – a man with two sons. One son was lost in the far country (like the sheep), but his father went to rescue him and bring him home to a party. His brother was lost close to home (like the coin), and his father went to rescue him too, but he refused to be rescued and come into the party. The self-righteous older brother knew he was nothing like his wayward younger brother, and yet in seeking to show the difference, he proved they were the same: both brought shame to their father, both wanted their father's wealth without their father's relationship, both preferred to party with friends, both needed their father to humiliate himself in order to rescue them. If the religious complainers were upset about Jesus partying with sinners, they would have been fuming by the end of this little tale.

The story of the lost sons underlines a key truth in Jesus' teaching. He was not so convinced about the 'good' and 'bad' distinction among the people. For Jesus, it wasn't about good folks also known as the religious elite, and bad folks who were the sinful riff-raff. The truth was that there were sinners who thought they were good and sinners who knew they were bad: All sinners – but sinners with opposite responses to Jesus. Jesus could comfort and confront both kinds of people in the same crowd with the shortest of stories. There was a moneylender, and he was owed five hundred denarii by one debtor, and fifty by another. He forgave both. Which loved him more? (Lk. 7:41–42).

Kneeling before Jesus as he told this story was a great sinner who loved him even more after she heard this simple tale of extravagant grace. And also in the room was a proud host who would have been profoundly offended by the story's implication – specifically, the implication that this woman (the uninvited visiting sinner) loved Jesus more than he did. More than that, there was also the unmissable statement that the host, a 'good' man, was still considered a debtor, that is, a sinner! It takes longer to spell out the implications of the story than to tell it!

Jesus did not simply tell stories to offend or to comfort. He was a master teacher too. One time a lawyer asked Jesus what he should do to inherit eternal life. Jesus turned the question back and asked him what he thought. It turns out this lawyer impressed Jesus by pointing to the need for love toward both God and neighbour. But then he wanted to clarify who his neighbour was. So, Jesus launched into another masterful story.

In reply Jesus said: 'A man was going down from Jerusalem to Jericho, when he was attacked by robbers. They stripped him of his clothes, beat him and went away, leaving him half dead. A priest happened to be going down the same road, and when he saw the man, he passed by on the other side. So too, a Levite, when he came to the place and saw him, passed by on the other side. But a Samaritan, as he travelled, came where the man was; and when he saw him, he took pity on him. He went to him and bandaged his wounds, pouring on oil and wine. Then he put the man on his own donkey, brought him to an inn and took care of him. The next day he took out two denarii and gave them to the innkeeper. "Look after him," he said, "and when I return, I will reimburse you for any extra expense you may have."

'Which of these three do you think was a neighbour to the man who fell into the hands of robbers?'

The expert in the law replied, 'The one who had mercy on him.'

Jesus told him, 'Go and do likewise'
(Lk. 10:30–37).

Notice that the expert in the law could not bring himself to identify who proved to be the neighbour in the story. You can almost imagine him clearing his throat: 'It was the Sam … the Samar … the one who had mercy on him.' His anti-Samaritan prejudices precluded the possibility that a Samaritan could be the hero of the story. Jesus had no problem presenting a foreigner as the generous and sacrificial hero of the story. After all, Jesus knew full well that he was himself the kind and generous-hearted rescuer who came from outside the situation and risked everything to sacrificially save those who could not save themselves. Meanwhile, for the expert in the law, the surface lesson was clear: your neighbour is anyone you encounter who has a need that you are in a position to meet. Go love them.

Jesus could tell stories to offend the religious, to comfort forgiven sinners and to train those who would follow him. As we read, learn and think about the stories of Jesus, we will find ourselves challenged, prodded, uncovered and undone time and again. Jesus' stories are not just for children, they are for us grown-ups too. Read them and let them saturate your soul – be continually challenged by the profound simplicity of Jesus: the perfect communicator!

A PASSAGE TO PONDER: LUKE 7:36-50

As you see the mini story of the debtor in its context, think about the emotions stirred in each character in turn: in the woman, in Simon the host and in Jesus.

In what ways can you identify with the woman, and in what ways can you identify with Simon? How does Jesus comfort and challenge you through this story?

A SONG TO SING

Come, Thou Fount of every blessing,
Tune my heart to sing Thy grace;
Streams of mercy, never ceasing,
Call for songs of loudest praise.
Teach me some melodious sonnet,
Sung by flaming tongues above.
Praise the mount! I'm fixed upon it,
Mount of Thy redeeming love.

Here I raise my Ebenezer;
Here by Thy great help I've come;
And I hope, by Thy good pleasure,
Safely to arrive at home.

Jesus sought me when a stranger,
Wandering from the fold of God;
He, to rescue me from danger,
Interposed His precious blood.

O to grace how great a debtor
Daily I'm constrained to be!
Let Thy goodness, like a fetter,
Bind my wandering heart to Thee.
Prone to wander, Lord, I feel it,
Prone to leave the God I love;
Here's my heart, O take and seal it,
Seal it for Thy courts above.

O that day when freed from sinning,
I shall see Thy lovely face;
Clothèd then in blood washed linen
How I'll sing Thy sovereign grace;
Come, my Lord, no longer tarry,
Take my ransomed soul away;
Send thine angels now to carry
Me to realms of endless day.

Robert Robinson, 1735—1790

THE MIRACLE-WORKER

For about three years, Jesus seemed to alternate between teaching in parables and performing miracles. Just as his teaching was perfectly targeted to two different audiences – one very favourable and the other much more antagonistic – so his miracles also polarised the populace into two groups. Just as we can easily misunderstand his teaching as being simple stories to communicate heavenly truths, so we can easily misunderstand his miracles as merely being proofs to authenticate his divine identity.

When we read Mark's gospel, we find Jesus performing miracles, but then repeatedly telling the healed person to keep it quiet and not spread the word (see, for example, Mk. 1:44–45 or 7:36). That is confusing. After all, weren't miracles acts of self-authentication? Surely Jesus needed to spread the word and let the social media buzz build a following for his messianic movement? Actually, no.

Jesus' miracles did underline who he was – he was the promised man from heaven who would bring God's great kingdom into this broken world. His miracles pointed to the eventual end of sin, the curse and death. But Jesus was wary of a cheap following. He did not want a crowd who were there only for a free meal, or to see the spectacle of a miracle. In fact, after feeding the five thousand in John 6, he says:

'I am the living bread that came down from heaven. Whoever eats this bread will live forever. This bread is my flesh, which I will give for the life of the world.'

Then the Jews began to argue sharply among themselves, 'How can this man give us his flesh to eat?'

Jesus said to them, 'Very truly I tell you, unless you eat the flesh of the Son of Man and drink his blood, you have no life in you. Whoever eats my flesh and drinks my blood has eternal life, and I will raise them up at the last day.

On hearing it, many of his disciples said, 'This is a hard teaching. Who can accept it?'

From this time many of his disciples turned back and no longer followed him
(Jn. 6:51–54, 60, 66).

Why did Jesus speak about their need to feast on him, the true bread from heaven, if his goal was to build a bigger following? His 'eat my flesh and drink my blood' speech spoke of the profound connection he had come to create with his followers, but his shocking imagery scared off the huge crowds. Was it a public relations disaster? Or was it Jesus making sure that he did not build a false following of miracle consumers?

The miracles of Jesus point us to God's kind heart. Many times we read that Jesus was moved with compassion and so made it possible for the hungry to eat, the lame to walk, the deaf to hear, the demonised to enjoy freedom, the blind to see and even the dead to live again. Even when performing a healing brought complications for his ministry, Jesus would still care for those in need. His compassion revealed the kind heart of God.

The miracles of Jesus also point us to God's greater mission. Even when the dead were raised to life, it was only a matter of time before they would die again. His physical provision pointed to a greater spiritual provision – spiritual sight, the ability to hear his voice, heavenly bread, the life of the Spirit and so on. The miracles of Jesus were merely a foretaste of God's great plan to bring an end to the nasty effects of the curse. One day, the dead will rise to live forever, the blind will see forever and the lame will leap forever. Jesus broke into the dark grip of sin and showed God's preferred future for humanity. Would people accept this help from outside?

Ultimately, the great confrontation was not just between Jesus and the forces of evil manifested in demons, disease and death. It was also a confrontation between the giving nature of

God and the grabbing grip of human autonomy. We do not like to be helped; we prefer to help ourselves. Just as Jesus was fixing the unfixable, so he also made it obvious where human hearts remained impenetrable. For example, time after time, we see Jesus performing a life-giving miracle on a Sabbath, the traditional Jewish day of rest. At times, as we read the Gospels, it feels like Jesus was biding his time waiting for another Sabbath so that he could wind up the authorities with another healing. Where the religious leaders should have been stirred with delight, they were instead resilient and hard, stubbornly hard hearted toward God's kindness (Mk. 3:1–6.)

The human heart is hardened toward God so that even when God breaks in and does immeasurable good, hardened hearts attribute that power to the devil himself. Jesus divided people then, and he still does today. We may not regularly see the kinds of miracles that Jesus offered as a foretaste of a heavenly kingdom, but Jesus still polarises people today. Speak of God and people will raise an eyebrow but typically tolerate your 'personal spirituality'. But mention the name of Jesus and hackles go up, then defences, and increasingly you will feel a backlash against you that is a taste of what Jesus experienced time and again.

People are often open to some generic spiritual force that some may choose to rely on – a helpful crutch to their superstitious and needy hearts. But personify the particular God of the Bible in the person of his Son and the offence levels climb sharply. In our humanness, we want to be mini-gods, dictating our own lives and even our own spirituality. We prefer not to believe that there is a particular God who is fully revealed in his Son, Jesus of Nazareth. It is offensive to our prideful hearts! Jesus performed life-giving miracles and yet was despised. He gives new and transforming life today and will continue to be hated for it.

How can the miracle-working power of Jesus mark my life today, especially if I don't see that power at work in my situation? Read Matthew, Mark, Luke and John, the four accounts of Jesus' life, ministry, death and resurrection. Pray for Jesus to intervene in life's darkest times, but know that we can live today with an energised anticipation of the day when Jesus steps into this dark world to banish darkness, disease and death forever. What if pain and suffering and grief and loss cannot grip us forever? What if every story of hurt has an end that is still to be written? What if we are walking with the one who not only has the power to make broken things whole, but who has the motivation to do so once and for all?

A PASSAGE TO PONDER: MATTHEW 14:13-33

Imagine being with Peter and the disciples as Jesus fed the crowd of people. How would being there affect your view of Jesus?

Imagine being Peter in that boat as Jesus approached and then invited you to walk on water and join him. How would that whole experience shape your relationship with Jesus?

A SONG TO SING

Praise, my soul, the King of Heaven;
To His feet thy tribute bring.
Ransomed, healed, restored, forgiven,

Who like thee His praise should sing?
Praise Him! Praise Him!
Praise the everlasting King.

Praise Him for His grace and favour
To our fathers in distress.
Praise Him still the same for ever,
Slow to chide, and swift to bless.
Praise Him! Praise Him!
Glorious in His faithfulness.

Fatherlike He tends and spares us;
Well our feeble frame He knows.
In His hands He gently bears us,
Rescues us from all our foes.
Praise Him! Praise Him!
Widely as His mercy flows.

Angels, help us to adore Him;
Ye behold Him face to face;
Sun and moon, bow down before Him,
Dwellers all in time and space.
Praise Him! Praise Him!
Praise with us the God of grace.

Henry Francis Lyte, 1793—1847

THE MISSIONARY

Jesus combined three main ministries during his three years of recorded action. As well as confronting the religious leaders, and caring for the broken and needy, Jesus focused on a third group of people – his disciples.

The disciples of Jesus were a motley crew that included among others, fishermen, a tax collector and a political zealot. They were not educated nor from elite backgrounds. Their accents would have been frowned upon by the cream of society. Their attitudes and actions have been frowned upon by generations of Christians sitting comfortably in churches down through the centuries. And yet this ragtag band of Jesus' followers would eventually turn the world upside down!

If they were not qualified for ministry based on their natural abilities, their academic prowess, or their personal strength of character, then what was it that prepared them to continue Jesus' ministry after he returned to be with his Father? They had been with Jesus. This was the key. They had been with Jesus and some things had obviously rubbed off on them.

For instance, if we were to walk with the disciples through Matthew chapters 8 and 9, we would experience some of the learning that would have come from being with Jesus.

When Jesus came down from the mountainside, large crowds followed him. A man with leprosy came and knelt before him and said, 'Lord, if you are willing, you can make me clean.'

Jesus reached out his hand and touched the man. 'I am willing,' he said. 'Be clean!' Immediately he was cleansed of his leprosy (Matt. 8:1–3).

We can use our imaginations to picture this leper approaching Jesus. How long had it been since he had known the touch of another human? How long had he been an outcast? How much had the reports of Jesus stirred hope within him? Perhaps we can imagine the moment when Jesus' hand touched the man, and the words of healing were spoken. But don't forget, the disciples were there too. They would have been filled with concern as the leper approached. Perhaps they dispatched someone to get behind the leper and signal to Jesus, making sure he knew not to get too close? Perhaps they gasped in shock as the hand reached out, and then pondered in quiet whispers that night as they recalled not only the healing but also the compassion of Jesus.

Jesus touching a leper was one moment among many similar incidents. Matthew's account continues with Jesus setting out for the home of a Roman centurion, presumably to touch his servant, then records Jesus touching the hand of Peter's mother-in-law, a sick woman. Lepers, Gentile servants, women…these were not the parts of society that the disciples would expect Jesus to reach out and touch. But they saw it and they gradually received their training in his ways of compassion (Matt. 8:1–17).

The disciples would have seen him address a violent storm with authority, then cast out the demons that were destroying a man's life, then grant forgiveness to a paralysed man (and heal him too, in order to give a more obvious example of his authority). They watched and they learned that this Jesus not only cares for the lowest of the low, but he also has the highest authority (Matt. 8:23 – 9:8).

Jesus' disciples would have closely observed the final group of healings in these two chapters:

- The pair of women who were desperate for healing; one was a 12-year-old girl who was probably used to having everything she wanted, the other was an unclean outcast woman with a 12-year-old problem (Matt. 9:18–34).

- A pair of men desperate to see (vv. 27–31).

- The man with the pair of problems: having a demon and being unable to speak (vv. 32–34).

Humanity's desperate need was painted vividly for the watching eyes of the disciples.

In these chapters, the disciples watched Jesus in action, and surely this apprenticeship with the Messiah had a powerful impact on their lives. Even today, as we spend time with Jesus, as we read the Gospels and walk with him through life, we too start to become more like him. So for the disciples there was a process going on, but there was also a crisis point. At the end of chapter 9, Jesus presented the crowds to them:

> *Jesus went through all the towns and villages, teaching in their synagogues, proclaiming the good news of the kingdom and healing every disease and sickness. When he saw the crowds, he had compassion on them, because they were harassed and helpless, like sheep without a shepherd. Then he said to his disciples, 'The harvest is plentiful but the workers are few. Ask the Lord of the harvest, therefore, to send out workers into his harvest field' (Matt. 9:35–38).*

Here was a great crowd of people with needs and concerns, fears and doubts, hurt and struggle. Perhaps with tears running into his beard, Jesus urged his disciples to pray for more workers to go into the harvest field. This crowd of people were like sheep without a shepherd, and Jesus wanted his disciples to catch and share his compassion for them. The next thing we read, in chapter 10, is that the disciples are being sent out to continue the ministry of Jesus. Perhaps this points us to the great qualification for a ministry like the master – spend time with Jesus and gradually you will receive his heartbeat transplanted into your inner being. With that in place, go and represent him to the hurting world around you.

What Jesus does here, sending out his disciples, he will do again at the end of Matthew's gospel. After deliberately training, teaching, sending, debriefing and sending again, eventually Jesus leaves his disciples with the Great Commission: I have authority, you go make disciples, bring them in and build them up, and know that I am always with you.

We find the same commissioning of the disciples going on in John 20:21–22. 'As the Father has sent me, I am sending you' (there is the authority and commissioning). He breathes on them and spoke much of the giving of the

Spirit (there is the 'I will be with you always'). In chapter 21, he carefully reminds them of their mission to be fishers of men and to feed the flock (there is the 'baptising them and teaching them to obey' – the bringing people in and building them up language of the Great Commission). How did Jesus remind them of their mission? First, he repeated the miraculous catching of fish with which he had first called them to be fishers of men back in Luke 5. Second, as he recommissioned Peter to be a leader within the church, he called him to feed the flock. At the same time, Jesus also taught Peter, who was still raw from denying Jesus, that failure is not final – a helpful lesson for us all! (Jn. 21:15–19).

Spending time with Jesus changed his disciples. Their hearts started to beat with his for the hurting and the needy. Then he gave them his Spirit and sent them out to turn the world upside down. Today we have that same Spirit, and we too can spend time with Jesus as we follow him in the pages of the Bible. What a privilege it is to commune with Jesus and, in the process, to be prepared and invited to participate in Jesus' great mission!

A PASSAGE TO PONDER: JOHN 20:19–31

It is so easy to take the resurrection for granted, especially if you have been a Christian for some time. Prayerfully place yourself in the sandals of those disciples and consider what seeing Jesus and hearing his words would have done in their hearts and lives ... not just that evening but for the rest of their days!

The last two verses tell us John's goal for us when we read his gospel. Pray that this would increasingly be true for you in the days to come.

A SONG TO SING

O for a thousand tongues to sing
my great Redeemer's praise,
the glories of my God and King,
the triumphs of his grace.

My gracious Master and my God,
assist me to proclaim,
to spread thro' all the earth abroad,
the honours of thy name.

Jesus, the name that charms our fears,
that bids our sorrows cease;
'tis music in the sinner's ears,
'tis life and health and peace.

He breaks the pow'r of cancelled sin,
he sets the pris'ner free;
his blood can make the foulest clean,
his blood availed for me.

He speaks, and list'ning to his voice,
new life the dead receive;
the mournful, broken hearts rejoice;
the humble poor believe.

Hear him, ye deaf; his praise, ye dumb,
your loosen'd tongues employ;
ye blind, behold your Saviour come;
and leap, ye lame, for joy.

So now Thy blessed Name I love,
Thy will would e'er be mine.
Had I a thousand hearts to give,
My Lord, they all were Thine!

Charles Wesley, 1707—1788

THE KING

Knowing the king of the universe is a wonderful privilege. Knowing that the king is humble is wonderful beyond words. The mission of Jesus was not just to draw near to us in the incarnation, or to instruct by teaching, or to care by healing, or to prepare his disciples by mentoring but the mission of Jesus was to die.

Some people think the statement 'God is love' needs to be balanced. God is love, *but also* God is wrathful, they will say. It is as if a declaration of God's love will leave him open to the charge of being soft and sappy. While it is nice to think only of God's benevolence, where would we be if God were lacking in strength and courage? Instead of trying to balance talk of God's love with a supposed counterbalancing attribute, let us instead do a better job of describing God's love. How can we best do that? By making sure our talk of God's love is always clarified by the cross.

Jesus set his face as a flint to go to Jerusalem. He knew that he would be rejected, beaten, unjustly tried and ultimately, executed. He knew how much the religious leaders hated him. He knew that they would have to hand him over to the Roman authorities to be tried, beaten and killed. He knew that the Roman conscripts would not be Italians, but most likely Samaritans who would love the opportunity to beat a Jewish messianic figure. He knew that death at the hands of Rome meant the excruciating agony of the cross – critical nerves on fire by piercing nails, every breath a ferocious ordeal to lift one's weight out of the drowning asphyxiation, and perhaps most of all, the absolute humiliation of nakedness. He knew all that. And still he set his face as a flint to go to Jerusalem (Lk. 9:22, 44, 51).

The beautiful attributes, or perfections, of God are seen in the Son heading for the cross. We see the love of God, and it is a love that drips blood-red. We see the glory of God, and it is a glory that is unreservedly self-giving. We see the humility of God, and it is a humility that takes us to the very core of who God is.

From a distance, we might ponder the cross and its theological meaning. The one who stood closest to the cross of Christ declared, 'Surely this man was the Son of God!' (Mk. 15:39) The whole of Mark's gospel builds to this climactic moment. The reader is told in the first verse that Jesus is the Christ, the Son of God. The people on the page don't seem to grasp who Jesus is. Then, when we arrive at the central hinge of the book, we finally hear one of Jesus' disciples declaring that Jesus is the Christ (Mk. 8:29–32). It took them long enough to get there, but Jesus was not satisfied with that declaration. He immediately spoke of the cross and his own death. Why? Because Jesus could not let them have a Christ without the cross. The Messiah was not just a miracle-worker; he was on a mission to die. It was only after Jesus died that the centurion announced the punchline of the book of Mark: 'This man was the Son of God!' It is only at the cross that we can see clearly and fully who Jesus is.

John's gospel also has a climactic punchline, and again it comes in a moment of clarity. On the third day, Jesus rose from the dead! The tomb was empty, and Jesus met with various disciples over the next weeks. A week after that resurrection day, Jesus appeared to the eleven disciples. This time, Thomas was there. Thomas had declared his unwillingness to believe unless he saw with his own eyes and touched with his own hands the marks of the cross on Jesus' risen body. So Jesus came and stood before Thomas. He didn't rebuke the doubt, but invited Thomas to touch him. Jesus wanted Thomas to be certain of his resurrection. Thomas then got to give the punchline to John's gospel – 'My Lord and my God!' (Jn. 20:28).

The resurrection of Jesus must be considered alongside the wonder of the cross. Death could not hold Jesus. As Paul reflected on the resurrection, he wrote:

> But Christ has indeed been raised from the dead, the firstfruits of those who have fallen asleep. For since death came through a man, the resurrection of the dead comes also through

a man. For as in Adam all die, so in Christ all
will be made alive. But each in turn: Christ,
the firstfruits; then, when he comes, those who
belong to him (1 Cor. 15:20–23).

Jesus stepped forth from the tomb as the firstfruits
from the dead. The firstfruits is a declaration
that more is coming. The great enemy has been
defeated and now, what do we have to fear? Not
even death itself!

'Where, O death, is your victory?
  Where, O death, is your sting?'
The sting of death is sin, and the power of sin
is the law. But thanks be to God! He gives us
the victory through our Lord Jesus Christ
(1 Cor. 15:55–57).

The death of Jesus is sometimes presented as a
good mission gone bad. Nothing could be further
from the truth. The death and resurrection of
Jesus was the good mission for the bad. Jesus
took on himself the penalty for our sin and paid
the price in full. He presented us with a love that
can overwhelm our self-love and bring us back

to God. Jesus gave himself for us, for there was nothing more valuable he could give. He could not have loved us any more. When the King was lifted up and exalted from the earth, he drew all people to himself. His moment of glory was his exaltation on the cross. The King was enthroned and his glory revealed – and what a glory it was!

With his mission accomplished, Jesus ascended to his Father's side, back to where he belongs. We would not be too far off if we imagine the Father saying, 'Well done, Son, you revealed my heart perfectly to all who dare to believe.' The sinner is now united by faith to Christ and brought into the closest relationship of them all!

We live our lives in the glorious shadow of the cross. It is only in kneeling before the cross that we can see God clearly, or anything else for that matter. We must not look past it, craning our necks for a more glorious glimpse of the ascended Christ. Instead, we look through the cross and discover that in heaven today, there is a wounded and scarred man. It is with our humble God in view that we can be transformed, and that we can see clearly once again. Not a day should go by without our visiting the shadow of the cross. Indeed, let's linger there, see clearly, worship deeply and so live devotedly.

A PASSAGE TO PONDER: JOHN 12:12–36

The crowds welcomed Jesus as their king, but they could not have anticipated what kind of king he would prove to be in the following week. Notice how Jesus' response to the request from the Greeks in verses 23–32 gradually reveals what kind of king and what kind of glory Jesus had come to show.

If the glory of Jesus is seen in the self-sacrificing death of the cross, what does that stir in your heart as you think about him? Maybe a song comes to mind to sing or pray to him? Maybe you want to write your own hymn or expression of praise?

A SONG TO SING

When I survey the wondrous cross
On which the Prince of glory died,
My richest gain I count but loss,
And pour contempt on all my pride.

Forbid it, Lord, that I should boast,
Save in the death of Christ my God!
All the vain things that charm me most,
I sacrifice them to His blood.

See from His head, His hands, His feet,
Sorrow and love flow mingled down!
Did e'er such love and sorrow meet,
Or thorns compose so rich a crown?

Were the whole realm of nature mine,
That were an offering far too small;
Love so amazing, so divine,
Demands my soul, my life, my all.

Isaac Watts, 1674—1748

THE BROTHER

Too easily we fall into the trap of thinking that Christianity is just a present faith in a past reality that makes for a better future. That is, Jesus was active two thousand years ago and will come again at some unknown point down the line. But what does this leave for the present? Just to believe and behave?

The problem with this thin version of Christianity is that the burden is completely on me. *I* have to choose to believe and *I* should be choosing to behave. But this is not the life presented in the New Testament. If we read John's gospel, we find that believers are like the branches abiding in a vine, or even participants in the you-in-me-and-I-in-you relationship of the Trinity (Jn. 15 and 17). If we read Paul, we find that believers are united to Christ because now, we are 'in him' (for example, Eph. 1:3–14). Peter's second letter tells us that we have already become partakers of the divine nature (2 Pet. 1:4). We could go on, but let's zero in on two shockingly profound terms for those who belong to Christ.

First, Hebrews tells us that Jesus is not ashamed to call us brothers (Heb. 2:11). By adoption, God brings sinners to share in the sonship of the Son. As brothers with Jesus, we get to share his relationship with the Father himself.

Notice what these two passages have in common:

For those who are led by the Spirit of God are the children of God. The Spirit you received does not make you slaves, so that you live in fear again; rather, the Spirit you received brought about your adoption to sonship. And by him we cry, 'Abba, Father.' The Spirit himself testifies with our spirit that we are God's children (Rom. 8:14–16).

But when the set time had fully come, God sent his Son, born of a woman, born under the law, to redeem those under the law, that we might receive adoption to sonship. Because you are his sons, God sent the Spirit of his Son into our hearts, the Spirit who calls out, 'Abba, Father.' So you are no longer a slave, but God's child; and since you are his child, God has made you also an heir (Gal. 4:4–7).

In both passages, it is the Spirit that stirs up within us a cry of '*Abba!* (Daddy!) Father!' This is not the hesitant approach of a subject to a distant authority figure. This is the bold access and confidence of a true son. Just as Jesus can speak to the Father at any time, so now we have that same love-driven, glory-giving relationship with God. We might be tempted to tweak the tenses and make this something we anticipate, but the text is clear – this sonship is ours now, today, present tense.

What is the present tense reality of this relationship from Jesus' perspective? Hebrews goes on to describe how the one who is not ashamed to call us brothers became like us in every way so that he could help us. He helps us by providing himself as a sacrifice for our sin, and he helps us when we are tempted (present tense). In addition, in the third and fourth chapter of Hebrews, the preacher goes on to describe how Jesus now offers us the rest he has achieved, and how we must not be disbelieving but lean wholly onto him. By the end of this section, we are encouraged to approach the mercy seat to find the help from God that we need in this life. Why would God do this for us? Because our brother, the high priest, is both great and greatly sympathetic to our weaknesses:

> Therefore, since we have a great high priest who has ascended into heaven, Jesus the Son of God, let us hold firmly to the faith we profess. For we do not have a high priest who is unable to empathise with our weaknesses, but we have one who has been tempted in every way, just as we are – yet he did not sin. Let us then approach God's throne of grace with confidence, so that we may receive mercy and find grace to help us in our time of need (Heb. 4:14–16).

The sermon to the Hebrews continues after a warning passage focused on the priesthood of Jesus. Do not miss Hebrews 7:25 – Jesus always lives to intercede for us. We can approach the Father in our times of need. Whether we do or not, Jesus does. He prays for us. Day after day. What a priest, and what a brother!

As well as having Jesus as our brother, we also have him as our bridegroom. We will look at this more in the next chapter, but for now, let's consider the present tense reality of this relationship too. Our union with Christ by the Spirit is best pictured by the relationship of a husband and wife. The language of marital union is found in many Bible passages, but ground zero is Ephesians 5:22–33. Looking to human marriage, the wife is to be like the bride of Christ in her submission to her bridegroom. The more intense instruction is for the husband – he is to be like Christ who loves, who gives himself up, who washes with the water of his Word, who nourishes and cherishes who cares for his bride as if she were his own body. And then at the end of the passage, Paul reveals that he is actually turning the image around. It is not Christ and the church that offer a picture for human marriage, but human marriage is a picture of that ultimate marital reality between Christ and his bride, the church.

It would be easy to picture our marriage with Christ as a future reality to anticipate, and we will do so in the next chapter. After all, many passages do point to the future coming of the Bridegroom to claim his bride and celebrate the marriage supper. But Paul is clearly seeing the marital reality as already in place for the believer. This means that we live each moment gripped by the grace of God revealed in Christ both in the past and in the present. Jesus gave himself for us back then, but he washes us with his Word today. He nourishes and cherishes us today, giving us the soil and the sunshine we need to flourish as his bride. He cares for us now.

Too often we think of 'Jesus past' or even 'Jesus future'. But the Bible repeatedly urges us to gaze on 'Jesus present', to relate with Jesus today and to experience the transformation that he brings about in our lives as we trust in him.

To picture this marital reality let's ponder the image of a married couple dancing. He holds her, and he leads. She holds on too, but she does not strive. She keeps her eyes on him and lets him lead the dance. Sometimes they dance faster, sometimes slower, sometimes perilously close to a pillar, other times safely in the centre of the dance floor. The couple will struggle when the bride decides her dancing relationship is based on her own responsibility. She may pull back, or push forward, but this is not how the dance works. She is not passive – after all, nobody can carry dead weight and make it look graceful. She is very much involved but never with an autonomous responsibility, always as a response to him. The Christian life is a lot like this. We learn to trust as we gaze on our Groom and let him lead us through life. He will patiently work with us. But this is not the end of the story, this is just the anticipation of what is still to come. Because, one day, we will no longer dance by faith; instead we will be face to face!

A PASSAGE TO PONDER: ROMANS 8

As you walk through this passage, make a note of everything that it says about the present reality of a Christian. What do we have because of the Spirit of Christ?

In addition to our present experience of life from the Spirit, we can also experience real assurance of God's love in this life. Which verses reassure you of God's love? Perhaps talk to God about that!

A SONG TO SING

Before the throne of God above
I have a strong, a perfect plea,
a great High Priest, whose name is Love
who ever lives and pleads for me.
My name is graven on His hands,
my name is written on His heart;
I know that while in heav'n He stands
no tongue can bid me thence depart.

When Satan tempts me to despair
and tells me of the guilt within,
upward I look, and see Him there

who made an end of all my sin.
Because the sinless Saviour died,
my sinful soul is counted free,
for God the just is satisfied
to look on Him and pardon me.

Behold Him there! the risen Lamb!
my perfect, spotless righteousness,
the great unchangeable 'I AM'‘
the King of glory and of grace!
One with Himself, I cannot die;
my soul is purchased by His blood;
my life is hid with Christ on high,
with Christ my Saviour and my God.

Charitie Lees Bancroft, 1841—1923

THE BRIDEGROOM

When Jesus told his disciples that he was going back to his Father, they were more concerned for themselves than they were overjoyed for him. So, in John 14 – 16, Jesus offers them comfort and hope. He begins with wedding language and then focuses in on the key person in any marriage – the Spirit who will create the union between the groom and his bride.

> *'Do not let your hearts be troubled. You believe in God; believe also in me. My Father's house has many rooms; if that were not so, would I have told you that I am going there to prepare a place for you? And if I go and prepare a place for you, I will come back and take you to be with me that you also may be where I am. You*

> *know the way to the place where I am going'*
> *(Jn. 14:1–4).*

Their hearts were troubled at the start of chapter 14, not just because Jesus was leaving, but because he had just predicted that they would soon fail to follow him. It may sound strange to our ears, but Jesus offers comfort using wedding imagery. In that culture, the groom would arrange the marriage and then head back to his family home where he would diligently prepare the best living quarters he could for his bride-to-be. They were already technically married by the betrothal, but they were not yet physically together. His departure would be sad, but thoroughly tempered by the joy of anticipating his return, for that would mean wedding bells and being together for the rest of their lives. We can slip back into our cultural concepts so easily, and perhaps this is why we miss theirs.

Keith Green sang a slightly humorous song that said, 'I can't wait to get to heaven, where God will wipe away all our tears. In six days you created everything, but you've been working on heaven two thousand years!'[1] No doubt heaven will truly be amazing! But even better than the celestial accommodation, we will be thrilled forever to see and be with Jesus our Bridegroom.

> *'When the Advocate comes, whom I will send to you from the Father – the Spirit of truth who goes out from the Father – he will testify about me' (Jn. 15:26).*

Jesus had told them he was going to prepare a place and therefore, he would also come again and take them to be 'with me where I am'. By referring to the Father's house with its many rooms, Jesus was comforting them with the language of a future wedding. So what does this mean for us today? We enjoy our union with Christ by the Spirit today – and by the Spirit, by faith, we set the eyes of our hearts on him and participate in that dance we thought about in the last chapter. But there is more, more now, and more still to come.

---

[1] Keith Green, 'I Can't Wait to Get to Heaven', *The Prodigal Son* (Sparrow Records, 1983).

We live in anticipation of his return. Just as the groom would go and busily build a home to live in, so the bride-to-be would be active in anticipation. The bride anticipating the surprise return of her bridegroom would be busy washing and preparing herself for his sudden arrival. Notice how John uses the marital anticipation again in his first epistle:

> But we know that when Christ appears, we shall be like him, for we shall see him as he is. All who have this hope in him purify themselves, just as he is pure (1 Jn. 3:2–3).

The bride of Christ is actively responsive to his lead in anticipation of his return in the flesh. We are told elsewhere that it is Christ who washes the bride with the water of his Word, who sanctifies us by his Spirit, whose grace teaches us to live self-controlled, upright and godly lives in this present age (Eph. 5:25–27; 2 Thess. 2:13; Tit. 2:11–13). And what is the active response of those who are gripped by his grace? It is to purify themselves. This is not a 'let go and let God' passivity. This is the eager response of a heart captivated by the Groom who is coming back for his bride.

One day, the wedding will occur. Christ will come back and everything will change. Interestingly, when we read about a wedding feast in the first three gospels, it is often tied to negative imagery rather than the glorious hope we might expect. Perhaps we could put it this way: the wedding will be both exclusive and expulsive. It is exclusive because only those who are his will be able to participate. Those who do not want to be his will not be allowed to participate. Why? Is it because God has to faithfully balance his love with his wrathful anger so that both realities remain true? Is God somehow balancing two contradictory characteristics? Not at all. It is because true marital love will always be exclusive and expulsive of all others. So, we read of weddings but also of non-guests being thrown into outer darkness where there is weeping and gnashing of teeth (Matt. 22:1–14).

To put it another way, the Bridegroom is coming to sweep up his bride into the embrace of the Trinity, and he is also coming to judge all that oppose God's great plan to do so. Questions will finally be answered. Wrongs will be made right. History will be completed. The Lamb and his bride will meet face to face.

You can read Revelation and get caught up in many details. You can trace the different understandings through the book. But the one thing we should all do is to allow the anticipation of that final wedding to stir our hearts:

> I saw the Holy City, the new Jerusalem, coming down out of heaven from God, prepared as a bride beautifully dressed for her husband. And I heard a loud voice from the throne saying, 'Look! God's dwelling place is now among the people, and he will dwell with them. They will be his people, and God himself will be with them and be their God. "He will wipe every tear from their eyes. There will be no more death" or mourning or crying or pain, for the old order of things has passed away' (Rev. 21:2–4).

> The Spirit and the bride say, 'Come!' And let the one who hears say, 'Come!' Let the one who is thirsty come; and let the one who wishes take the free gift of the water of life (Rev. 22:17).

Since the future is not just a pipe dream for religious folks but a reality ready to burst into our world, should that not influence the way we live today? Absolutely. And the key issue today, as it has always been, is how we relate to Jesus the Son of God. We all have two options: either we can be part of rebellious humanity preparing for a futile battle with God, or we can be part of the bride preparing for the breathtaking welcome into the heavenly presence of the glorious love of the Trinity.

Which option would you choose? Have you accepted Christ's proposal to turn to him, trust him for forgiveness and life, and receive the gift of God's love? If you already have, then how is your life today changed by anticipating being with Jesus on that day?

A PASSAGE TO PONDER: EPHESIANS 5:22-33

This passage is describing the marriage of Christ and the church (and therefore giving guidance for human marriages that reflect this greater marriage). What does it say about what Christ, our husband, does?

And what does the passage say about the response of the bride to her husband? Is that a good description of your response to Christ? If not, don't focus on trying harder to respond well, just take more time to think about all that Christ has done and is doing!

A SONG TO SING

The sands of time are sinking,
The dawn of Heaven breaks;
The summer morn I've sighed for –
The fair, sweet morn awakes:
Dark, dark hath been the midnight,
But dayspring is at hand,
And glory, glory dwelleth
In Immanuel's land.

O Christ, He is the fountain,
The deep, sweet well of love!
The streams on earth I've tasted
More deep I'll drink above:
There to an ocean fullness

His mercy doth expand,
And glory, glory dwelleth
In Immanuel's land.

O I am my Belovèd's
And my Belovèd's mine!
He brings a poor vile sinner
Into His house of wine.
I stand upon His merit –
I know no other stand,
Not e'en where glory dwelleth
In Immanuel's land.

The bride eyes not her garment,
But her dear bridegroom's face;
I will not gaze at glory
But on my King of grace.
Not at the crown He giveth
But on His piercèd hand;
The Lamb is all the glory
Of Immanuel's land.

Anne Cousin, 1824—1906

THE REST
OF THE STORY

What is heaven like? People tend to answer this question with town-planning descriptions – gold-paved streets and perfect surroundings. But this really misses the point. The point is that things that we value in this life – like gold – will be no more important than tarmac. We'll pave the streets with it! The real treasure is Jesus. He is what makes heaven so precious.

Heaven would be hellish for people who don't love Jesus. It makes no sense for God to offer some universal gesture of benevolence so that everyone gets to go there. Many people do not want to be in a world where they are not the centrepiece. Many who love the treasures of this world might be excited about a nice world full of treasures like gold or health or comfort. However, they would be sickened to be forced into a world where Christ is the captivating focus, where love for God and others is the oxygen of life. Heaven would be deadly to untransformed hearts, because self-oriented, in-curved hearts would be instantly choked by the lack of their preferred air and burned up by the brightness of God's self-giving glory.

Most of us have pondered what heaven will be like. The Bible pushes us away from the philosophical idea of a disembodied cloud-float and perpetual hymn-singing. Instead, it gives the impression that we will get to experience life as it was intended to be lived, on a curse-free new earth with no death, no rebellion, no corruption and no perversion. Surely we will delight to live, to learn, to travel, even to work in such an environment. But this is all incidental in comparison with the main feature of heaven.

If eternity back before the creation involved the Father delighting in and gloriously pouring out his love for his Son, and if the font and focus of history has been the man, Christ Jesus, then why would eternity be centred around anything or anyone other than him?

In his sermon on 1 Corinthians 13, Jonathan Edwards famously described heaven as 'a world of love'. It is the place where God's way is unchallenged and where loving others and putting them first is the only natural way to be. We get a glimpse of it in John 17, where Jesus speaks of the loving, glory-giving relationship between Father and Son. Intriguingly, Edwards points out that Jesus will forever continue to reveal the Father's heart to us. We won't know everything at once, and we won't ever completely grasp how good God's heart is ... but Jesus will forever continue to reveal the unseen Father to us. An eternity of discovery sounds infinitely rich – especially when that discovery will be ever greater depths of the good, good heart of God himself.

Without the antagonistic pressures of the world, the flesh and the devil, the Spirit's role of pouring out God's love into our hearts and pointing us toward Christ will be experienced to the full (Rom. 5:5; Jn. 16:13). Try to imagine that the Spirit of God will be able, with maximum bandwidth and without the slightest hint of hindrance, to assure us of God's love and make Jesus attractive to us. Jesus, without the slightest obstacle, will be able to continually reveal more of how good the Father really is. And we will be free to respond with a glory-giving love that we have only momentarily tasted at the very best of times in this life.

Our forever-future is focused fully on Christ, because Christ has always been the focal point of God's good plans. He has been rejected repeatedly throughout world history and throughout your personal history and mine. Despite this, Jesus gave himself fully to his Father's loving plan to provide a rescue and to draw our straying hearts back to his perfect love. And it is Jesus who will forever be the object of our fascination and our delight. If the Son of God has thrilled the Father's heart for all eternity, how could we ever imagine that he won't be everything we could ever ask for in our eternal future?

A PASSAGE TO PONDER: JOHN 17

Look at how the word 'glory' is used in this passage. Notice how it is given from one person to another. What emotion does Jesus feel as he speaks of glory?

Carefully read verses 20–26 again: try to imagine, or even to draw, the movement of glory and love between God the Father, God the Son and us. How much is flowing down in our direction? See how little is described flowing from us to God.

A SONG TO SING

Love divine, all loves excelling,
Joy of heaven to earth come down;
Fix in us thy humble dwelling;
All thy faithful mercies crown!
Jesus, Thou art all compassion,
Pure unbounded love Thou art;
Visit us with Thy salvation;
Enter every trembling heart.

Breathe, O breathe Thy loving Spirit,
Into every troubled breast!

Let us all in Thee inherit;
Let us find thy promised rest.
Take away our love of sinning;
Alpha and Omega be;
End of faith, as its Beginning,
Set our hearts at liberty.

Come, Almighty to deliver,
Let us all Thy life receive;
Suddenly return and never,
Never more Thy temples leave.
Thee we would be always blessing,
Serve Thee as Thy hosts above,
Pray and praise Thee without ceasing,
Glory in Thy perfect love.

Finish, then, Thy new creation;
Pure and spotless let us be.
Let us see Thy great salvation
Perfectly restored in Thee;
Changed from glory into glory,
Till in heaven we take our place,
Till we cast our crowns before Thee,
Lost in wonder, love, and praise.

Charles Wesley, 1707—1788

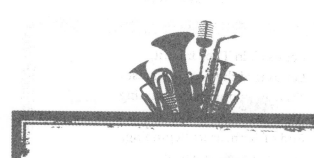

BE THOU MY VISION

Some years ago, C.S. Lewis suggested that Jesus must be either a liar, a lunatic, or else he is the Lord. This is certainly true, but the truth goes so much further than that. Jesus is not simply divine by a process of elimination: in other words, if he is not a liar or a lunatic, then Lord is the only remaining option. This is certainly true, but Jesus is so much more than just someone who 'ticks the boxes' to be qualified as God.

A generation after C.S. Lewis, Christians were asked 'What Would Jesus Do?' It is certainly true that we will never find a better example to follow than Jesus, but he is so much more than an example to us.

Jesus has forever delighted the Father, and now the Father invites us, by sending his Son and his Spirit, to enjoy all that Jesus is and has alongside him. The good news of Christianity is not simply that there is a way to pay for the guilt in all of our lives. Jesus gives us much more than a legal loophole. He gives us himself!

The Father so loved us that he gave his Son for us. The Son so loved us that he shared his relationship with his Father with us. The Spirit wants to convince our hearts that the delightful communion of the Trinity is an embrace that reaches out even to us. The invitation is not simply to have our sins forgiven but to be united by the Spirit with Christ himself. The good news certainly includes a legal component, but it is so much more. It is a true union, it is marriage, it is sonship, it is friendship and it is brotherhood. Everything Jesus has can be ours because Jesus gave everything he had for us. Jesus is such good news. He wants to be, now and forever, the captivating vision of our hearts!

A SONG TO SING

Be thou my vision,
O Lord of my heart!
Naught be all else to me,
save that thou art;
Thou my best thought,
by day or by night,
Waking or sleeping,
Thy presence my light.

Be thou my wisdom
and Thou my true word;
I ever with Thee
and Thou with me, Lord.
Thou my great Father,
I, thy true son,
Thou in me dwelling
and I with Thee one.

Riches I heed not,
nor man's empty praise;
Thou mine inheritance,
now and always;

Thou and Thou only,
first in my heart;
High King of heaven,
my treasure Thou art.

High King of Heaven
my victory won
May I reach heaven's joys,
oh, bright heaven's sun.
Heart of my own heart,
whatever befall,
Still be my vision,
oh Ruler of all.

Eleanor Hull, 1860—1935